I'd like to thank the following publications for previously featuring work from Sweet Tooth.

The Big Brick Review ("Fourplex")

aaduna ("Powder Blue")

Le Mot Just ("Peacocks")

Brain, Child ("Thirteen"),

Mothers Always Write ("Batman's Mom")

Laundry Literary Magazine and Doubleback Review ("How to Style Your Hair")

Light Ekphrasis ("Shortwave")

Mused Literary Review ("California Dreaming")

Lilac ("Wings" and "Cinnamon Girl")

SWEET
TOOTH

SWEET
TOOTH

Christine Green

PART ONE

INTERLUDE

PART TWO

To mom and dad, with love.

PART ONE

FOURPLEX

Today on the phone my mother says, "When we were land-lords . . ."

"What do you mean 'landlords'?"

"Your dad and I built a fourplex in Colorado Springs when you were just a baby. Those apartments were supposed to make us rich."

"You never told me!"

"Oh really? That's odd."

Usually, when my mother relates some story or memory that I don't remember she becomes annoyed at me, *"I've told you this a hundred times, honey."*

But today is different. When I ask her why she never mentioned it she says it was so long ago. It never came up.

To me, though, it is a big deal. The imagined life I had forty-one years ago in Colorado suddenly changes. I realize this is dramatic, but now I *have* to conjure a picture of this fourplex, of the tenants, the walkway, and the yard. I *have* to sit down with my eyes closed and imagine this place into my memory. I *have* to create the scene.

This is what I see: Four apartments, two on the first floor and two on the second. The exterior is stark white stucco, and there is clean snow in the front yard. All four windows are framed by black shutters and have closed curtains. There is a parking lot barely big enough for six cars. Just inside, in the shared hallway, there is an orange shag carpet. A gold and yellow hanging lamp dimly lights the entryway. The stairs to the second floor are on the left of the hall and there is an ironwork handrail. Directly across from the front entrance and down the hall is a back door with a red "EXIT" sign glowing over top of it. This door leads to a minuscule back yard that dips down into a steep, weed-filled ravine. Behind the ravine the woods rise up to the mountains toward Pike's Peak.

My mother tells me that three tenants are friendly. She then tells me that the couple in the fourth apartment is loud and dirty, and there is a foul smell lingering in the hall outside of their door. When they move out they leave the place trashed, and my parents break their backs cleaning the apartment.

The whole endeavor is more than they can handle. Mom and Dad don't have time to deal with the responsibilities of being landlords. They sell the building.

"I wonder if it is still there." My mom ponders out loud.

I wonder, too. I wonder if I can go there now and see the shag carpet and meet the tenants. Can I go to them and shake their hands and cry a little and theatrically exclaim, "My parents built this apartment! This is part of my history!"

Perhaps they would say, "Oh yes! I remember that nice young couple with the newborn baby. They were so charming."

Or would they ask me to leave and say they could care less who built the place? Would they say that it just doesn't matter? Would there be new tenants who are younger than I am and who would look at me like I'm a crazy old fool?

Maybe the place doesn't even exist anymore. Maybe there is nothing there but a dirty patch of snow.

POWDER BLUE

I am in my living room in my childhood home sitting
cross-legged on the floor and looking at old family photos.
I pick up a Polaroid of a blue Ford Pinto. I instantly recall
sitting in the backseat, my little legs stuck to the leather
on a hot day. My parents have told me that they owned
this car when I was very, very small. So small, in fact, that I
shouldn't remember ever riding in it much less ever having
seen it.

But I am not convinced, not entirely anyway. In my mind's
eye I am speeding down the highway in that car with my
family, my mother's long hair flying in the wind. None of
this ever happened, of course, but as I hold the picture in
my hand, I really believe it did.

The Polaroid Pinto is Powder Blue.

The fact that it is Powder Blue (and not Royal Blue or Navy
Blue or Steel Blue) is important to me for some reason.
It makes the only-in-a-photo car more real, more present
somehow.

Powder Blue.

I like the way the words feel as they pass my lips. I can
almost taste them on my tongue, soft and chalky.

But of course, there is nothing in my mouth. The taste is a

phantom one, an imagined one, like the false memory of a family car ride down a sunny California highway.

THE TENDER YEARS

1. I win a small plastic giraffe as a prize at school. It has a rainbow swirl of colors twisting through its body, and I am instantly in love with it. I accidentally drop the little animal behind the dresser in my room. I reach my arm underneath, but I cannot grasp it. I strain and struggle, yet I simply cannot will my arm to stretch any farther. I can see the giraffe tilted on its side just beyond my fingers. Its rainbow colors are muted and dull in the dark space under the dresser, and it feels as if my heart is about to break.

2. I'm sitting in the classroom, crying, in the arms of my teacher. The rest of the students are outside at recess, and I can see them through the open back door of the classroom. The teacher is soothing me and telling me to stop crying. What she doesn't understand is that I cannot help it. I simply do not know how to stop. The anxiety and sadness I feel has no explanation, thus it has no cure. I am a despondent little thing.

3. Everyone in the class is settled down for nap time. No one sleeps, though. We are a group of squiggly, wiggly, giggly worms. But we try. We really do, because if you are quiet and still and good the teacher may tap you gently on the shoulder. This muted signal lets you know that you get the first choice of toys at playtime. I am desperate for my teacher to pick me, because I badly want to play with the

little plastic eggs in the toy refrigerator. They nestle sweetly in a plastic carton and when one is "cracked" a perfect yellow center is revealed. I need to play with those eggs, so I struggle to be as still as I can. I squeeze my eyes shut, and I know in my heart that I will be chosen any minute now. But when the lights go on, and I open my eyes I see that I am not special.

4. I am sitting on the front step of my house. It is a beautiful, sunny day, and I am enjoying being alone. It is the weekend, and I am relieved to stay home from school. My mother brings out a tray with my plastic tea set. She gingerly sets it down beside me and shows me that the pot is filled with Kool-Aid, a treat we rarely have. I am delighted. I fill a cup and carefully walk to our snowball tree. The boughs are heavy with flowers, and they hang down in such a way as to create a perfect room under the branches. I sit there watching the world through a gauzy white veil.

PINE-SOL: A TRIPTYCH

Pinus Sylvestris

Pine Oil

Odor: Strong, fresh, grassy, balsam

Emotional response: Cheerful, stimulating, rejuvenating

Color: Clear or light golden yellow

Consistency: Thin

Pine essential oil is used as an ingredient in homemade and commercial cleansers and disinfectants, as a chest and nasal decongestant and/or expectorant, for general respiratory support, and to uplift and invigorate the senses.

In 1929, chemist Henry A. Cole of Jackson, Mississippi created Pine-Sol cleanser using pine oil extracted from the stumps of dead pine trees. His invention was extremely successful, and by the 1950s Pine-Sol was one of the most popular household products in the United States.

Much to the chagrin of its customers, Clorox (the Pine-Sol parent company) discontinued the use of authentic pine oil in Pine-Sol in 2016. Devoted consumers were so angry that thousands signed a Change.org petition demanding that the company continue using an 8.75% dilution of pine oil in their beloved Pine-Sol.

Now die-hard scrubbers can purchase "Original Pine-Sol" online only. Pine-Sol products sold in stores contain no pine oil whatsoever. Their original catch phrase is: "Cleans—Disinfects—Deodorizes."

Mama

I'm sitting in the front yard and the sun is so bright that it hurts my eyes. My mother and sister are with me, and we're washing toys in big silver tubs filled with soapy water and Pine-Sol. There is an illness to recover from, to wash away with the garden hose, so that it doesn't re-infect the children or spread further among the household. It is fun, sitting in the sun on the grass, among the pansies, lathering frothy pine-scented water into my Barbie's hair. My mom is smiling— her teeth are so white and straight— and her brown skin is completely smooth. There are no blemishes or wrinkles or freckles. She must be tired. Sleep was lost in tending sick kids; and now, there are so many toys, even stuffed animals, to scrub and bathe until the skin on our hands is tight and wrinkled. We pass a bottle of Jergen's lotion among us to soothe our puckered skin as we sit quietly on the grass, squinting at the clouds.

How to clean your bathroom

Pour two capfuls of Pine-Sol in the toilet. Wait, make it a ¼ cup. Or just pour straight from the bottle until the scent stings your nose, just a little.

Use a toilet brush to scrub the bowl vigorously until there is no ring at the waterline.

Next, tip the brush up under the rim as best as you can until you are sure it is clean.

Flush.

Flush again.

Pour a capful (or so) of Pine-Sol onto a rag and soak with steaming hot water.

Wipe the outer bowl and the base of the commode. Thoroughly clean the seat and tank, paying close attention to the handle. Use a clean rag or a paper towel to polish and dry the entire outer toilet.

Get another steaming rag with Pine-sol and clean the sink and counters, too. Use your fingernail or an old toothbrush where needed.

Pour more Pine-Sol in the bowl before leaving the bathroom, so that the scent lingers as you clean the rest of the house.

Wash your hands using mild dish soap and dry roughly before lathering with Jergen's original cherry-almond scent lotion.

Throw wide the windows to let the breeze ghost in and carry the fragrance of pansies into the bath room. Close your eyes as you long for your mother and her sleepy smile and water-wrinkled hands.

PEACOCKS

Peacocks scream in the night, and I think they are suffering.
I want to know if birds shed tears.

But all I spy when I peek out of my little girl birdcage are
iron bars and a steep hill with stiff grass, brown and crackly.

When the dry brush catches fire
all that remains is a wet blackness.

But I still hear them.
Wingless

I stare at the smoky scar and dream of
their gold and blue feathers sparking in moonbeams.

MIRROR

On my television there is a boy—probably about twelve—standing on a gray and stony Bay Area beach.

"I'm proud to be a Mexican-American!" he declares, fist pumping in the air as the ocean breeze ruffles his sweatshirt.

I stop everything when this public service announcement comes on channel two. I get right up close to the T.V, so I can watch him intently and soak up every word. My mom always tells us that we should be proud to be Mexican and American.

"But we aren't from Mexico," I always say, confused.

I don't yet understand about moving borders, about wars that put families first in one country and then another, about the Southwest and the borderlands.

This proud boy appears on TV once, maybe twice a day. But after a minute or two he is gone and *The Brady Bunch* resumes and they are so blond and have a maid and a two story house and their parents let their dog inside. I watch Marsha and Jan and Cindy because that is what is offered. I swallow the images and covet their pink ruffled room and attached bath.

I wait patiently through *Petticoat Junction* reruns and *The Andy Griffith Show* for the Mexican-American boy to return to the screen, so he can teach me how to be proud.

SUGAR BABY

Your mom is hot, man.

We look out the window at my friend's mom. Her long
brown legs in a white tennis skirt draw all eyes her way as
she pumps gas. We stand there in the convenience store,
with Charleston Chews and Sweet Tarts clutched in sweaty
fists, stunned that these men with tattoos and cigarettes
hanging from their lips are talking to us. We just came in
for sugar.

Really, dude, she's hella sexy. I mean, look at those legs!

We laugh. No one told us how to react when men scare
us, when they reduce our mothers to a pair of legs. No one
taught us how to walk away. All we know is how to giggle
and eat sweets.

To be sweet.

To smile, and nod, *yes.*

We have not yet learned that no is an option.

1995

I walk the long seven blocks from my apartment to my
job in the predawn dark. The streets should be empty, but
they never are. Men (so many men) doze on sidewalks,

wave hello as I pass. They serve up soft whistles, mumbled offers, and outstretched hands. I jut out my chin and pull my shoulders back convinced that I look like a badass, like I could take on whatever is put in my path. But every time I safely reach my destination, I let out the breath I've been holding for half a mile, half a lifetime.

LULLABY

*You have some creamy thighs smile mama damn you wearing
those jeans aren't ya how about a a drink whatcha doing later
call me baby anytime where you going bring me with you nice
skirt I like plaid want a ride can't you just stop and talk for
minute don't be so mean talk to me look at me I'm a good guy lets
chill you have any Irish in you want some I got some candy for
you little lady don't look so scared I won't bite unless you ask hey
turn around I'm talking to you think you're too good to talk fuck
you bitch*

CŌĀTLĪCUE*

People said my Nana had a green thumb but this made no sense to me when I was a child. Her hands were deep brown and her nails always red. They click-clicked when she flipped a hot tortilla on the comal or drummed her fingers on the kitchen table or deadheaded withered blooms from bleeding hearts.

The story goes that in the 1950s my Nana planted flowers in a dry pond in her backyard, turning an eyesore into an oasis.

When I was twelve, I wanted my very own garden, so my mother bought me a flat of yellow marigolds. I chose a sunny spot in front of the house near the carob tree. I dug and dug, not knowing exactly what I was doing, but I had plenty of enthusiasm. My trowel found an empty space in the ground, and before I could make sense of what was happening, a mass of snakes crawled over my hands. My screams brought Nana running to my rescue.

She beat back the dragons with a shovel that instantly turned into a magical sword and protected me from imminent death. The heroine had won the epic battle, and the surviving serpents retreated to their lair, defeated.

Cōātlīcue is the Aztec earth goddess who wore a "skirt of snakes."

Our hearts beat wildly before our hysterical laughter took hold of the moment. My mom thought we were being attacked by a maniac and came running outside, eyes wide. No, we told her, the underground things are just coming up for air. Then we laughed again because marigolds are supposed to repel snakes.

Sometimes, when I am puttering around my own garden, I pretend that I am with her at the old pond digging with gloveless hands.

I am no longer afraid of snakes.

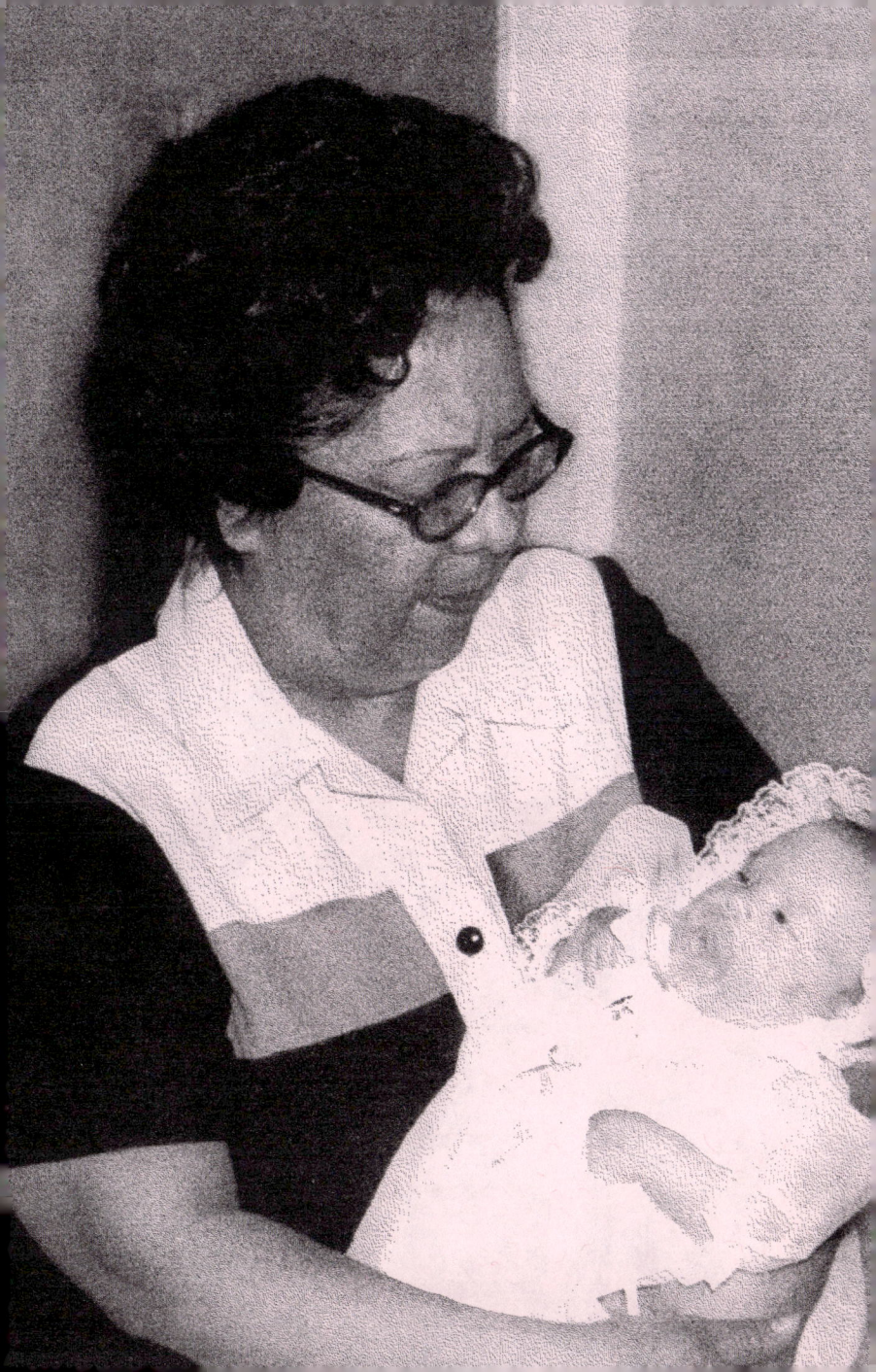

HOLY

Once, in about fourth grade, a weeping statue of the Christ child came to our church from Mexico. It was traveling, like a rock star, to different churches so the faithful could catch a glimpse of his sanctified tears. I don't remember his exact story or when he began to weep. I only remember that he came to us, to me.

I was a student in the adjoining Catholic school and we were allowed to visit the sanctuary during recess if we wanted to see the miraculous statue for ourselves. I went alone. It was cool in the church, and I sat in a pew near the altar. The statue looked to me like nothing more than a doll dressed up in a satin and lace baptismal gown propped up by a metal stand. But I knew he was special, the priest and the teachers told us so. He would cry, they said, and a lucky few would get to see his tears roll down his smooth porcelain baby cheeks. I willed his little blue eyes to cry just for me. I wanted to be special.

Two old ladies knelt in another pew and said their rosaries, and I felt guilty because I forgot the right way to properly pray a rosary, and mine was tangled at the bottom of my jewelry box anyway. The baby Jesus would probably not cry for someone like me who was just a dumb sinner.

I decided to kneel like the old ladies to see if that would

help. I stared as hard as I could into his doll face. I silently begged him to squeeze out one drop, one glistening bit of moisture. But he would not cry for me or those women.

I guess we just weren't holy enough.

SHORTWAVE

My father took out the short-wave radio on hot summer nights. They were the kind of nights when we played in the pool for hours past sunset and the grown-ups barbecued Italian sausages and hot dogs. The kind of summer nights when the neighbors walked around the fence to share gossip and cold beer.

Once we came across a strange radio broadcast: every few minutes a female voice reciting non-sequential numbers, then a pause, then a shrill, mechanical "beep-beep-beep." Repeat.

I later found out it was a "numbers station" broadcast by an unknown government agency so that international spies and little girls wrapped in damp terry cloth sipping Fresca could receive their orders.

Why can we only use the radio at night, Daddy?

He said something about the ozone layer, but I preferred to believe that the stars helped the transmission spread around the world like celestial mirrors reflecting the broadcast back to the tiny people of earth.

Last summer, while camping, my kids found a numbers station on our hand-crank radio. I pressed my ear to the speaker and heard my dad laughing between the beep-

beep-beeps, and I could smell wet concrete and grapefruit soda underneath the campfire smoke.

Grandpa Bob would have loved this. He would have loved you.

Tell us about him.

Listen to the radio, he is there in the static.

He is reaching out through the radio waves.

FIRE

Denise and I would lounge against the side of the liquor store while Jeremy and Travis skateboarded around the shopping plaza. We'd eat Jolly Rancher Fire-Stix that would turn our pouty teen lips red and sweet. Once we tried to dye Travis's dark, thick hair blonde by dousing it with pure hydrogen peroxide right there in the parking lot while Jeremy held the skate boards. It didn't seem to work, so we went back to eating our candy while the boys sailed around concrete curbs and over sidewalks. I wanted Travis to be my first kiss. At night, I dreamed about cinnamon lips and skateboards under the California sun.

MATH

Two days after my sixteenth birthday, the earth shook, and I thought I would die.

I sat at the giant oak table in my kitchen. The lights were off, and the afternoon sun dipped low in the sky. Shadows engulfed the room. On the stove, a large pot of soup simmered in preparation for dinner later that evening. A textbook thick with fractions was open on the table, and I read the same equation over and over until I had to rub my eyes and rest my head on the open pages. The glossy white paper cooled my cheek and sleepiness tugged at my eye lids.

Instead of napping, I raised my head and resumed my homework, carefully copying the equations on lined paper. Without warning, my chair rocked ever-so-slightly.

I lifted my eyes to look at the hanging lamp above the table. It swung back and forth with so much force that the edges of the wicker shade hit the stucco ceiling.

Earthquake.

In grade school, we'd practice earthquake drills like kids in other parts of the country practiced fire drills. We'd dash under the desks with hands clasped behind our heads,

41

elbows squeezed tight to our little ears. But I didn't usually worry too much about my ears. My biggest concern during those drills was whether or not my plaid uniform skirt adequately covered my rear end, so that whatever boy crouched under the desk behind me couldn't catch a glimpse of my panties. Despite the fact that I didn't take these drills too seriously, I did somehow retain the knowledge that the safest place in an earthquake was under a piece of heavy furniture. Heavy furniture like the large, oak table I sat at with my math book at that very moment.

When I heard a cry from upstairs, I flew up the stairs with uncharacteristic speed and lightness never even considering sliding underneath the table and covering my delicate ears. When I reached the top, I saw my mother in the doorway to her room, my Nana in her doorway, and my sister in hers. I stood firm under the lintel at the top of the stairs.

It was a common perception, once upon a time, that a doorway was the strongest part of a building. School teachers told us that in the absence of a sturdy piece of furniture one should stand in a door frame. Unfortunately, this outdated "fact," is wildly untrue. How many people around the world stood in doorways, clutching the woodwork during an earthquake, thinking that they were safe? Screaming.

A smashed mirror.

Only about six seconds had passed since I first saw the lamp swing violently against the ceiling.

More screaming. Hands outstretched to each other. We couldn't reach.

Eleven seconds.

Later, when my friends and I told each other our stories of the Big One, everyone joked about how fun it was. "What a ride!" But not me. I knew, absolutely knew, I would die in that moment while I watched the women I loved shake and wail in terror and shock. We would die. I was sure of it.

Fifteen seconds.

Stillness. Quiet. A merging of bodies and quiet sobs.

"Are you ok? Are you hurt? Sit down. Take a deep breath."

We were intact.

When we were sure our feet were steady, we went outside. Everyone else in the neighborhood was out there as well.

Necks craned skyward as if the shaking came from the clouds and not the earth beneath the cracked concrete.

Next, we piled in the car and drove around East San Jose to survey the damage. We didn't need anything as we still had power (miraculously) and plenty of food. Yet we had this intense need to see what had happened and who was out there. We cruised ever so slowly by houses and stores, staring. People were lined up outside of grocery stores and pharmacies to buy batteries and canned food.

Somewhere on Highway 17, my dad sat on the roof of his car with hundreds of other stranded drivers, and watched the sunset over the cities below. Commuters, trying to cross the mountain pass from Santa Cruz to Los Gatos and San Jose, found themselves stuck in traffic for hours. Someone passed out cans of soda. They worried about their families and thought of the dinners that they were late for while city lights twinkled below the mountain.

They waited.

We waited.

My mother still can't say why she made such an enormous amount of food for just a family of five, yet it fed friends and neighbors all evening. Nothing was wasted.

Eventually, my father came home. My parents embraced like they had been separated for years instead of hours.

There was no school the next day or the day after that, and the TV was on constantly, flashing pictures of broken bridges.

I never finished my math homework.

❧ ❧ ❧ ❧

67 PEOPLE DEAD

OVER 3,000 INJURIES

$5 BILLION IN DAMAGES

EPICENTER: LOMA PRIETA PEAK IN SANTA CRUZ, CA

MAGNITUDE: 6.9

INTERLUDE

EVERYONE'S FAVORITE NO-BAKE DESSERT

"Someone should bring Jell-O. You know, something innocent on the stomach."

She said this when the women were sitting around the
table planning who was to bring what dish to the funeral
supper the day after my dad died. They made lists of who
would bring slow-cooked pots of beans and pans of enchi-
ladas and trays of lunch meats and cheeses. And everyone
knew, of course, that random people would just show up
with an assortment of salads and cakes and pies.

But she said we needed "something innocent," too. Something that wouldn't upset our tender, grieving stomachs
that ached and lurched at even the thought of a cold turkey
sandwich slathered with mayo.

I was on the couch listening, or rather, trying not to listen,
when I heard her that first time. Then she said it again.
And again. No one was really paying attention to her,
though. She was one of those people that liked to insert
herself in situations where she wasn't needed or, like in this
case, wanted. She was here as a hanger-on who came in
someone else's car with a plate of cookies and a couple of
kids.

She was that person that ends up at every family affair
whether it's some prissy aunt, a cocky spouse of a guest, or

a loudmouth second cousin. It doesn't matter their relation to the family. They are just there trying to be more important and more needed than they really are.

When she showed up no one cared, not really. What was one more mom and a few more children at that point anyway? After a death a house is filled to the brim with people and for those deep in the muck of grief it doesn't always matter who is there. We just needed the white noise of a busy house — the dishwasher running, someone unloading groceries, kids opening and closing doors looking for snacks and toys, people making calls to florists, and the women (always the women) planning and cooking the food.

Her voice pierced that soothing background noise like the buzz of a chainsaw.

Something innocent.

I wanted to scream and tear at her face and her hair. I wanted to tell her that no one here was innocent anymore.

I didn't make a sound, though. I just curled up tighter into myself and covered my ears and tried very hard not to think about Jell-O.

CINNAMON GIRL

Aaron stroked my hair as we reclined in bed and listened to Neil Young's "Cinnamon Girl." I pretended that he was thinking of me, but I knew he wasn't. Somewhere in the past, before there was an "us," there was another girl, the Cinnamon Girl. I was just a replacement. A "for right now" girlfriend.

I wanna live with a Cinnamon Girl

I could be happy

The rest of my life

With a cinnamon girl...

Somehow, "for right now" turned into almost two years.

My friend Noelía didn't like him. This should have been a clue, a warning. Instead I took it as jealousy that I was partnered and she was alone. Of course, this was only my arrogance and vanity. She saw what I did not. He wasn't good for me. He was unkind and rude and cocky.

An example: Once I called him at his house and it was clear from the background noise that he and his room-mates were having quite the party.

"Stop calling, bitch; I'm with my boys."

When he talked to me like this, when he was a jerk to my

friends, when he talked down to me for not being as smart as he was, I let it go. Because when we were tangled in each other's limbs and his hand found that place at the small of my back that made me melt I thought we were meant to be together forever. I mistook pleasure and the warmth of a body next to me in bed for love. At these moments I told him I loved him. I told him that I wanted a life together. He only changed the subject or got up and left the room. He never responded. He never told me, "I love you."

One December night I tossed my schoolbooks in my backpack and walked to his house up the street. We were planning to study for finals, eat some canned tomato soup, watch some TV. The path to his house was dark and crowded with bushes and scraggly trees and shadowed houses. I felt a pleasant sense of aliveness the way the young do when evening falls and the night is blooming black and possible. Some women might have been afraid of what lurked behind tree trunks and in doorways, but I had very little fear of the streets. I was oblivious to the dangers of the world.

 When I got to his place, I sat down on the dirty, orange couch and emptied my school books onto the coffee table. It was such a college-boy apartment: filthy bathrooms, beer cans everywhere, greasy dishes in the sink. I always felt a little grossed out in that place. His one roommate, Brian, was a frat boy who was silly and loud but gentle and kind. His other roommate was a bodybuilder and ate nothing but meat and rarely wore a shirt. There was a third roommate, too, Mark. He and his girlfriend, Angie, always shared their pot and pizza.

That night, Brian was on the phone, pacing around the kitchen. He came into the living room and said that my mother called on the other line. I needed to call her back right away.

"Why would my mom call here?" I thought. I didn't even remember giving her their number.

When Brian finished his call, he handed me the phone. I felt my boyfriend behind me, his breath on my ear as I dialed. A family friend answered, and I was instantly confused and frightened.

When my mother finally picked up the line, I was ready for the worst. And it was the worst. Between sniffles she told me, "Daddy died."

I crumpled. Just like in a movie or on TV, I received the bad news and fell right to the floor.

Aaron helped me into Mark's car and buckled my seatbelt for me, because my hands were numb. When we got to my own apartment, my roommate was already tearfully packing my suitcase.

Angie and Aaron took seats beside me on the futon like bookends. I just sat there, sobbing. Noelía was at the kitchen sink doing my dishes, her back to all of us. She was crying, too. I could tell by how her shoulders shook. She was wearing her favorite brown sweater.

Angie and Mark drove Aaron and me to my parents' house. The drive was silent except for my sniffling. I smoked a cigarette and wiped snot off my face. I looked out the window and realized that boogeymen lurked in every corner. Nowhere was safe.

A few weeks after the funeral, when the semester was over and Christmas was near, Aaron came with me to my parents' house. We had no plans to get a tree or decorate in any way. He convinced us that we needed to try, that perhaps getting a tree would cheer us up. He herded me, my younger sister, my mom, and my grandmother into the car and we went to the nearest Christmas tree lot.

I stood among the Norway Pines and Blue Spruces and Balsam Firs and watched my mother walk in and out of the rows of trees, silent except for the occasional heavy sigh. My sister was stock still while she looked off into the distance, towards the clouds. My grandma clutched her purse with both hands and tried to smile as she inspected different trees.

Aaron finally helped us find one. He dutifully loaded it into the car, carried it into the house, and set it up in the stand. He was trying so hard to lighten the mood and ameliorate our grief. But sadness hung in the air, a choking smoke from a dead fire. We were smothering.

We decided that if we had to have a tree, we should at least take a different approach to decorating it. Traditionally we used hundreds of colored lights, a rainbow in every branch. But that year we went with plain white ones. We all sat there staring at the finished tree. Aaron stood next to it, proud that the tree was finally lit, and that he had brought us all together around it. But I couldn't bear to look at those lights. I stared past the tree through the gauzy curtains to the street. I looked towards the drainage canal to the east. I couldn't quite see that far, but in my mind's eye I imagined a snowy egret standing there poking his head into the muddy water to pluck out a fish. The stark lights cast a glare on the window and my eyes burned. I shook the fog from my brain and turned to Aaron. I felt done, empty. He rose to the occasion and helped me through those dark days, and I was grateful. But I also knew that things needed to change.

After that day I no longer envisioned a future for us. He became my "for right now" boyfriend.

Winter turned to spring, and I somehow rallied enough amidst my grief to graduate, to apply to graduate school, to make plans to move. I didn't ask him to come with me. I didn't ask him to try the long-distance thing. I just got ready to go.

We spent some quiet days together at the end of the summer camping, shopping for my new place on the east coast, sitting in silence.

When it was time to part, we stood in the train station and said our good-byes. I was too tired to cry anymore. I'd been crying since December, and I was weary.

He stood there with his skateboard in one hand and his backpack in the other, and his blond curls fell over his blue eyes as he mumbled, "I love you."

It was barely a whisper, but I didn't ask him to say it again. I didn't pound his chest and ask him why he waited so long to say it. I didn't beg to know about the Cinnamon Girl.

I simply turned and walked away.

A dreamer of pictures, I run in the night

you see us together chasin' the moonlight...

THE AGE OF INNOCENCE

When my father died, I was convinced he had suffered a violent death. Minutes after I received the news, I was swept up in the journey home. I had no time to ask "how." As I sat in the car watching the black night blur by, I imagined horrible scenes of his death:

A serial killer broke in and murdered him as he sat at his desk.

He was in a car accident so horrific that his body was severed in several places.

He was hit by a stray bullet as he stumbled upon a robbery at a 7-11.

But the truth of it was this: A heart attack so massive that it stopped him in his tracks as he was leaving his favorite bookstore during his lunch break. He died clutching a copy of Edith Wharton's *The Age of Innocence*.

For months after his funeral, I dreamed about all of the violent ways a person can die. Murderers. Accidents. Monsters.

There was always blood. In the movies, people wake from dreams like these with a start. They sit straight up in bed screaming and shaking. The sheets are twisted and they shiver with a cold sweat. They cry. My waking was never so dramatic. I would simply open my dry eyes and stare at the ceiling. No screaming, no tears. I would stay perfectly still until the ugly death-scene dissipated, and I could move my limbs and get out of bed.

※ ※ ※ ※

About one year after his death, I had a very vivid dream.

I am standing in a train station. No one is around except a man in a trench coat and fedora. It is my father. He walks to me and leans over to kiss my cheek.

"I have to go now," he says.

He boards a train. The doors slide closed, and I wave as it departs leaving a puff of steam in its wake.

I didn't wake up afraid and paralyzed like after the nightmares. This time I woke up sobbing with tears soaking my face and hair and pillowcase.

The bad dreams are gone, mostly. Sometimes I go to the bookstore and find *The Age of Innocence*, but I never buy it. It is simply enough to hold it in my hand.

PART TWO

SISTERS CALL

(After Rick Moody)

Sisters call their vacationing parents from a phone in their grandmother's farm house in Missouri. They try not to cry, but the little one, only three, can't help it.

I need a red ribbon, she says, her curls bobbing as she sobs. The grandmother climbs up to the dusty attic to find a perfect red bow.

Sisters call their grandmother, a year later, from California.

We miss you! Come soon!

Their small hearts ache for this far away grandma. They learn early that they can send love across telephone wires and in hand-written letters. Distance cannot diminish affection.

Sisters call California from Missouri again, but this time they are years older.

It isn't really that bad, they say. *Just a few stitches, really.*

But their mother knows that it is more than a simple scrape. She can hear the quiver in her youngest child's voice as she assures her, *I'm fine, Mommy, I promise.*

Sisters call boys and their school friends and always want to be on the phone now that the teen years have come. They carry the giant cordless phones from room to room and their parents discuss a second line just to avoid hassles and arguments.

Sisters call each other only occasionally now since the older one moved away to college. They are occupied with school, work, and friends, so there just isn't time anymore. In fact, the phone takes on an increasingly smaller and smaller role in both of their busy lives.

Sisters call a little more often after they become separated by an entire country. One now lives in the east and the other remains on the west coast. Still, they are busy and only talk now and then when time allows.

Sisters call more often now to discuss wedding plans.

But you have to choose a color, the youngest tells her older sister as they plan for a September wedding.

Ok, ok, um, blue. Just pick any blue dress. I wish Daddy could be there to walk me down the aisle.

Sisters call constantly now that a baby is on the way. On the day of the birth the youngest calls the hospital in a worried panic about the delivery.

Her big sister tells her, *I'm ok, everyone is ok. It's a girl! Can you be her godmother? You'll be her tía, her nína, her special auntie.*

Sisters text:

I'm on the bus and this guy I am sitting next to looks just like your husband! LOL

Are you watching the presidential debate? I mean who is this bozo?

I'm so jealous that you are at the beach again! I miss SF. Xoxo

I think I'm pregnant.

Sisters call because texting about babies and pregnancies just isn't enough.

I can't wait for you to be a mommy, too!

I love you and I'm so happy, she says, to her no-longer-a-baby-sister. I love you so much. Forever.

Sisters call each other sobbing with worry about their mother who is in the hospital so far away. They ache with worry and love and curse the miles, because while the distance doesn't weaken the love they have for each other and their mother it makes everything so damn hard.

Sisters call and hand the phones to their toddlers and small children yelling, *Say hi to your tía! Don't press the buttons! Just sing that song you learned at play group for tía and your cousins.*

They ask for advice about teething and homework and laugh and cry about how crazy and hard and wonderful it is to have these little people in their lives.

Sisters call and say, *I miss you.*

Come back to California.

Come to New York.

I miss you.

I love you.

I miss you.

AGENESIS

What does it mean to have no wisdom teeth?

I never developed those prehistoric third molars yet my empty sockets are questioned, doubted.

No one believes that I should be so lucky or so odd. Why is the absence of something that should not be there in the first place unusual?

Those cruel molars often send adults back to their cradles to a time when, with their chins wet with drool, they wailed for something hard, raw, sinewy to chew: a mother's finger, a plastic rattle, a wet towel.

My husband had all four of his wisdom teeth pulled just two weeks after the birth of our son. He writhed with pain in our big bed while I nursed the toothless, squirming baby in the nursery.

The baby and I just rocked to the sound of the soft rain; both comfortable in our mouths, no sharp edges ripping through gums. Just soft sucking, drowsy lullabies.

What wisdom comes of this?

CALIFORNIA DREAMING

"Do you miss it?" A friend asks, casually.

"California? Yes. Yes, I do."

I miss the palm trees and the rainy winters and the mountains. But I miss the beaches most of all. I crave the crashing cold waves, the sand dollars, the sea lions, the fishy air, the sharp little broken shells, and the tangles of seaweed.

My kids will not have a childhood where they regularly see a quail bob its silly head among a field of orange poppies or see a rose bloom in February. They'll never see a ghost town in the high mountains or have a cactus grow in their own back yard. They'll never pick a lemon right from a tree or grow avocados or bushes of rosemary so big they rival any eastern boxwood. They'll never see a sage bush bloom is the desert. They'll never try to wrap their tiny arms around a thousand year-old tree.

Instead they wrap coats tight around their growing bodies for most of the year while they hunch their shoulders to protect their hearts from the cold. They get their vitamin D tested yearly and wear heavy snow boots everywhere they go from December to April. They don't see the sun for much of the year, and they sleep in fleece and flannel and use so many blankets and comforters they look like tiny dolls in toy cradles.

My daughter asks about California often. "I want to see the ocean."

I look in her eyes and, despite the fact that she has only been to California a few times in her young life, she feels the same pull that I do. That tugging that turns you west and drags you toward the Pacific has a hold on her. My son's blood runs with the ice and cold of Western New York, though. He builds snow forts and runs around barefoot in the dead of winter. He loves the gray coolness of Lake Ontario. When my girl and I look west his eyes turn north to the lake, to an icy wilderness I have no desire to explore.

So, my daughter and I cut out magazine photos of vast California beaches and redwood trees. We dream of the Sierras and the ocean and a different life: a life of rosemary bushes and salt air and flowers in February.

THIRTEEN

Last week my daughter asked me to help her edit and
revise some poems she wrote for class. The theme was
a rather advanced one: the Bosnian refugee experience.
She is anxious and a little sad by nature, and I sensed her
nervousness. I didn't want to upset her so I chose my words
carefully. Usually, when I help her write, she becomes
prickly and uneasy, quick to be offended by any suggestion
I make. But not this time. She listened as I critiqued and
nit-picked and corrected. She even smiled, I think.

She worked on the poems for the next couple of hours
despite the fact that there was no school the next day and
the rest of the family watched a movie and ate popcorn and
dozed on the couch.

I read her poems the next morning. I didn't ask permission
and felt a little ashamed about that. They were good but
sad and dark. I felt proud and confused and heart-achy. She
can channel so much sadness and beauty in just a few lines
of eighth grade poetry. Her melancholy and anxiety trans-
mutes to art that is incandescent. This child, this girl-wom-
an, is such a different animal than I was so many years ago.

Thirteen, 1986: I am small, much smaller than most of
the girls in my class. My white uniform shirt falls limp-
ly against my chest. I don't need a bra but wear a trainer

because you can see right through the flimsy polyester. Knees, knobby and sharp, poke out from underneath my plaid skirt. I wear my hair short, which is a huge mistake. My thick, straight tresses look best when I leave them long. But a picture in some glossy magazine convinces me to cut if off. I look weird.

I am reading books I've taken from my father—Flaubert and Saki. My science teacher catches a glimpse and asks if I really understand what I'm reading. I do understand and tell her so. She believes me, and I tuck the books away feeling embarrassed but not entirely sure why.

I may be smart, but I am naïve beyond words. Once I am asked to light the candles on the class Advent wreath. The idea of lighting a match terrifies me, and my natural anxiety peaks to panic. When the flame ignites, I hastily drop it . . . right on the pine wreath surrounding the purple candles. The teacher looks at me with disbelief. It is clear that she—and the rest of the giggling class—think I am ridiculous for not knowing how to light a match. I *feel* ridiculous. But my soul is all air and water. My head is filled with Ideas and Notions. My heart is somber and easily bruised. I am quick to cry and am continually scared of the world. I can't even use the stove at my house. I rely on others for heat.

She got an A on those poems as I knew she would. But I worry about all that sadness. It's a sadness tinged with anger, confusion, and nervousness. She is too young to be so somber.

This makes me think that the coming years will be hard, much harder than I am ready for. Already we can come at each other with an intensity that startles me.

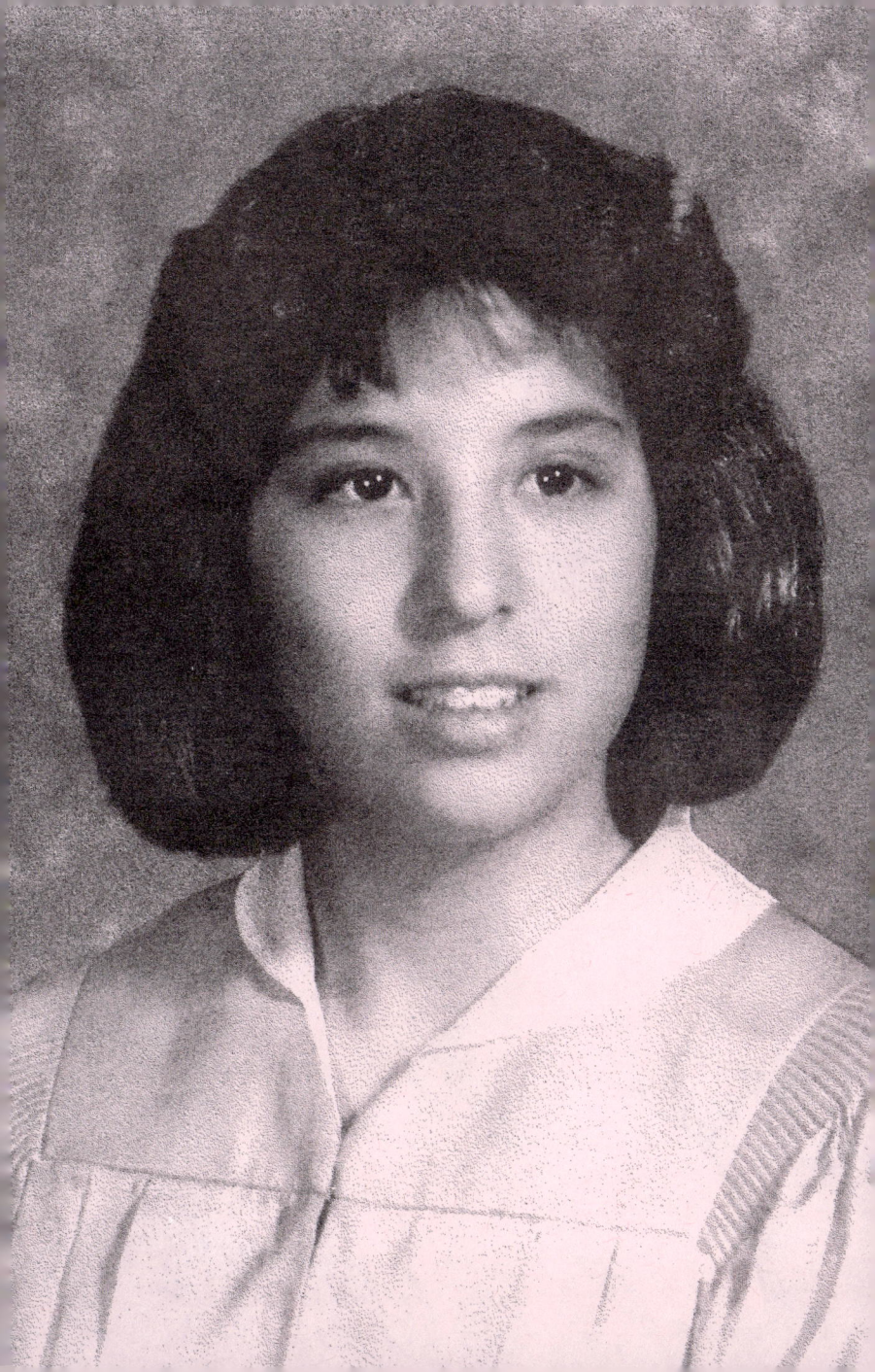

I cry. She yells.

Water. Flame.

Steam.

❃ ❃ ❃ ❃

Thirteen, 2014: She is fire through and through. She can light a match, of course. And she can bake bread and walk home from school alone. She wears black and doodles on her sneakers. She hates gym class and is a voracious reader. Books litter her room, and I often find them tucked in her bed sheets and even in the laundry basket. No magazines, though. Fancy fashion spreads hold no interest for her. Instead she studies Shintoism and researches the ins and outs of cardiac surgery. The affairs of the heart fascinate her on every level. She thinks about heaven and death and loss and takes on the sorrows of the world. Those sorrows are tinder for a blaze of anger that glints in her hazel eyes when she tilts her head.

She talks back and mouths off and teases her little brother. She has perfected the eye roll and slams doors in such a way as to shake the whole house.

Sparks fly.

She is so hotheaded at times I want to douse her in cold water. Occasionally, when she is walking in the snow, I watch the steam rise from her heart and finger tips and the tip of her nose. I watch it rise into the ether and mix with the stars.

CARTOGRAPHY

It is late winter in Western New York, and I feel chilled from another snowy, dishwatery day. I long for San Jose. But it has been twenty years, and so little of that old life remains. My family has moved as has most of my friends. I have children to care for and work to do, and travel isn't an option right now. So I embark, instead, on the most modern of journeys: Google maps.

A few key strokes, ENTER, and I am there again.

The 1965, 1,100 square foot yellow ranch has transformed into a 2,000 square foot white and red two-story house. The tall, protective redwood fence surrounding the front yard is gone. Someone has lifted and extended the porch and added stairs.

I switch my gaze to the left and the neighbor's house is exactly as it was in the seventies. It is the same watery turquoise with white trim and a canopy of palm trees and tropical plants shading the yard. I wonder if the people I remember from my childhood are still there? Do they still have those giant parrots? Do they still have a pomegranate tree?

I scroll around to our other neighbor's house. It is a blur. Google has muted the picture so that I can not see anything but the fences to the right and left and the two big carob trees in the front. I used to collect their brown pods and peel out the seeds. I remember hearing that people would eat carob, and I'd thought it so odd that anyone would eat these stinky, brown, dead-looking husks.

I look back at my old house. It is as if the entire home I grew up in has been torn down and replaced. The window I once looked out of into our front yard is gone as are the iron bars that striped my view. There is no more snowball tree, no more giant jade plant, no more swing set.

I decide to take a look around the neighborhood, so I move my mouse around the street corner. Every curve and bend feels familiar and good, and that shaky feeling I felt when I first saw my old house settles a bit. But suddenly, as I am "walking" down Story Road, I am lost. I've veered off onto a different street, one I don't remember and am not familiar with. I try to retrace my route, but I only get more confused.

I close the browser and take a deep breath. I can't go home, not really. I have no idea who owns that house now, and I'll never walk through that door again. I won't ever again buy candy at the Quick Stop, and I'll never eat my neighbor's pomegranates while sitting on the sidewalk listening to their squawking parrots.

I flip the laptop closed and look out the window. The icicles are dripping, just a little, and I decide to slip on my snow boots and take a walk down the street and around the corner.

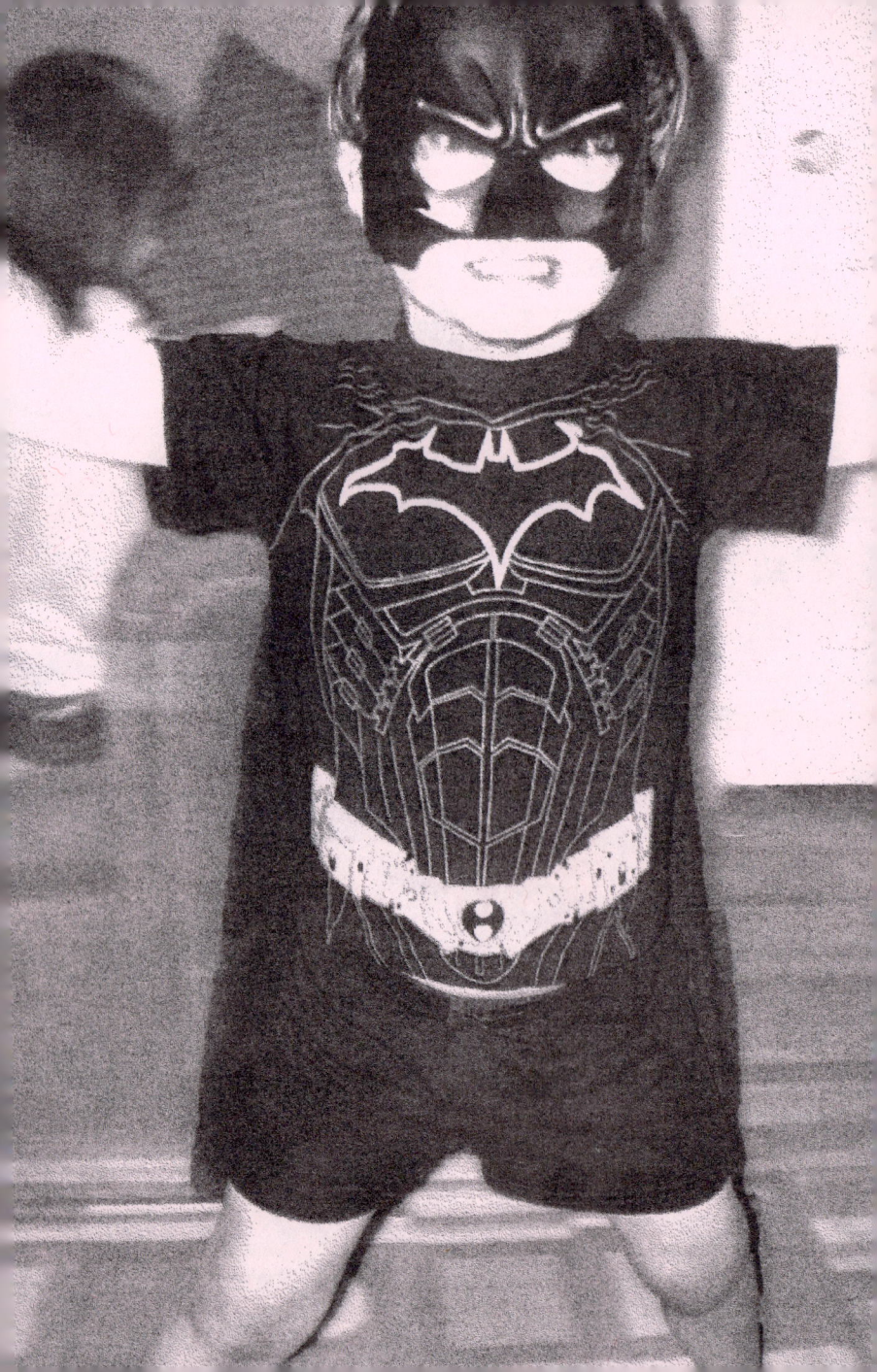

BATMAN'S MOM

"Marvel basically sucks and your friend is just plain wrong. DC comics are far superior, man."

Asking Ethan which was better, Marvel or DC, was supposed to be a quick question. I should have known better.

"I mean come on, Batman is basically the BEST, and most altruistic superhero there is. Jesus, Spiderman is just a dumb kid. "

"Ethan, you are just a kid, too, ya know. You're only twelve."

But it was clear he was on a roll. I sighed and rubbed the spot on my neck where earlier today a knot had formed during a phone call with a coworker.

"Ok, so I admit the Marvel movies have been better in recent years, but the DC comic books blow Marvel comic books clean out of the water!"

I looked at him, and he was on fire. This wasn't silly to him. This was something he really thought about. He cared about this. I suddenly wanted to hug him and touch his spiked hair.

"Dude, I mean, there really is no point arguing with a Marvel fan," said Ethan.

There is no point arguing with a DC fan either, I thought, as a smile pulled at the corner of my mouth. Damn I love this goof ball boy.

"Come on it is so obvious DC is better! Duh."

Where does he get this stuff? Why does everything become a speech instead of a simple answer? I did reach out and hug him then. I smelled his goopy gelled-up hair and wanted to kiss him on the ear like when he was a baby.

Thank God he is mine. Thank God he is my boy.

He pulled away then but not before squeezing me hard around my soft middle. He grabbed his cell phone and reclined on the couch again, a tangle of limbs that seemed so long all of a sudden. It was like his bones had stretched far beyond their normal little boy length all in the time it took for him to rattle off why DC was superior to Marvel. I stood at the doorway and watched his eyes dart from cell phone to TV and back again. His one hand hung off the edge of the couch to pet the dog.

Did Batman have a dog? I wondered. I knew Batman didn't have a mother, and the thought made me melancholy.

He was changing so fast. It was overwhelming to see skin tighten over jawline and feet outgrow shoes at a rate that was beyond even the toddler years.

His doctor had also noticed the rapid change. And something more, too.

The pediatrician felt there was something just a little off with his back. To him, Ethan's spine seemed a bit "crooked." He sent us to a scoliosis specialist.

The orthopedics office buzzed with efficiency and before

long several nurses had measured and scanned and poked at his tender hips and sharp shoulder blades. The doctor walked in the examination room with a flourish and immediately started joking with his young patient like they were old buddies. He made my son walk back and forth, bend over, stand on one foot. He pulled up the x-rays on the computer and studied them, silently, for a long minute.

"He doesn't have scoliosis. No, his one leg is just longer than the other."

The doctor said all of this as he pointed to the black and white image on the screen. My child's spine glowed liked a Halloween skeleton, and it made him seem at once vulnerable yet strong, grounded.

"See, his longer leg just tilts him to the side a bit so that he lists like a wobbly table."

I thought of sugar packets then, about how people stuck them under shaky table legs to get them to stand straight and firm once again. Maybe if I fed him sugar from a spoon like a baby bird his shorter leg would catch up to the other. Maybe I could fix this.

"But it isn't a big deal actually. Almost everyone is like this. He is unmistakably normal. Go have fun and play outside and be a kid. There is nothing wrong."

Nothing wrong.

I remembered that doctor's visit while I watched his bare legs stretch across the couch. The fine blond hairs on his shin glowed a little in the blue TV light, and I imagined that the hair was baby soft like the down on a newly hatched robin. But I knew if I touched it it would feel just a little coarse, so I didn't reach out.

By the time Bruce Wayne—the most famous of DC's comic book heroes—was twelve, the age my son is now, he had been motherless for two years. When young Bruce was only ten, a criminal named Joe Chill accosted his family as they walked home from a screening of *The Mark of Zorro*. Chill killed Mr. and Mrs. Wayne, leaving Bruce alone and traumatized. He had no mother to stroke his hair or take him to doctor appointments. She wasn't there to witness him transform from little boy to adolescent to teenager to man.

Did Batman lean to one side when he was twelve? Does he lean to one side now? Does one of his clunky black boots have a small heel lift to help him stand straight as he fights crime and attempts to avenge the loss of his parents?

These thoughts flood my mind all at once, and I leave the room so Ethan won't see my tears. I don't want him to see me cry with nostalgia and love and grief over the loss of the Waynes. I want him to read his comic books (DC of course) and play with the dog and do his homework. I want him to stand tall and proud even if he does lean to one side.

SEASIDE

I dream of birth, messy and painful. I am watching a young
woman in labor. She is on a bed in a small room in a trailer
home. It is night and the window above her is wide open.
The breeze blows the gauzy orange curtains back and forth.
There is a midwife, a woman in her fifties who is thin as a
stick. Her skin has the deep wrinkles of a smoker who also
likes to turn her face to the summer sun. She has an assis-
tant who is quiet and unassuming. Her face is hard to see
but a sheet of messy dishwater hair drapes over her eyes
as she watches the mother to be. Without much pream-
ble, the baby crowns and the dark hair is wet and streaked
with bloody mucous. The midwife looks at her helper and
they exchange a look, a knowing. Soon enough a baby boy
emerges slippery as an eel. He is passed, squalling and
squirming, to the mother's chest. I know that if I were to
enter the scene and sniff the baby's head it would smell
like the ocean, like ancient seashells. The midwife opens a
wicker box. Somehow, I know this is for the placenta which
she will take with her when it is all over. I know she will not
tell the mother that she is taking her organ away for her
own use.

The next night, another dream: A friend hands me her
baby girl. The baby is about seven months old and her skin
is pale as cream, her eyes dark blueberries. She stretches

her mouth into a wide, moist smile when she looks into my eyes. She is not mine, but I bring her to my breast where she suckles happily. I feel warm and pleasant, the familiar coziness of oxytocin flooding my system. The child stops for a moment, and I ask her mother if I can continue. She cheerfully agrees. The baby greedily takes back my nipple. We nestle into the soft cushions of a heavy sofa, content. Outside of the dark room, the ocean swirls against a rocky gray cliff. I sit with my friend and her daughter, silent next to the sea.

HOW TO STYLE YOUR HAIR

At age four, let your mother take you for a short haircut. It will be a wedge in the back with a middle-parted bob in front ala Dorothy Hamill after the 1976 Olympics. Done.

But your hair will grow quickly. By first grade it will be very long. Do not wear it down, never let it flow; do not let it brush your shoulders as you play. Your mother will plait tight braids against your head. The braids will be so snug that nary a stray hair will escape for at least two days. If braids are not pleasing, or your mother feels a change of pace is necessary, pigtails or a high, secure pony tail will suffice. At night it is important to massage your scalp with your tiny fingers to relieve any soreness.

Beware, the middle school years will be awkward. Cut your hair in seventh grade. The celebrity styles you see in your mother's *People Magazine* will encourage you. Try a short style with feathery sides and just a bit of front fringe. It may not be quite what you expected.

Get a perm.

Get the perm straightened after Ernie Fierro and his cronies laugh at you in the schoolyard.

High school. Seemingly overnight your hair will become lush and long. It is truly amazing what hormones can do.

One day you will look in the mirror and see a young woman with thick, straight, shiny brown hair extending past her shoulders. There is power in this. Never wear your hair back in a ponytail or braid again if you can possibly help it.

Prom, of course, is an exception. French twists look good on you, so go for it. Tease your bangs.

Don't worry too much about changing hairstyles until college. Right before you move into the freshman dorms, chop your hair right to your chin. Let go of the mile-high bangs. It's okay if you are disappointed, if you feel a little less pretty, a little less powerful. By the end of the first semester it will be quite a bit longer. One thing the women in your family do well is grow hair.

When you are in your twenties, you'll be an archaeologist working in the hot Virginia sun. Really, now, there is no choice but to sweep your hair off of your sweaty neck. Your best hairstyle will be a simple bun. Do this: grab a pencil from the site's tool box. Twist up your long hair and use the pencil to secure a tight bun. Be surprised when the site supervisor, a fellow graduate student, tells you years later (when you are his wife) that he saw you do this and that he found it alluring and beautiful and seductive.

A few months after your wedding, go ahead and chop it all off. It's okay; just do it. Now doesn't that feel good? It certainly won't be as scary as you anticipate. Everyone is shocked and asks "why" but be assured that you look pretty cute.

In your second year of marriage, take a trip to the Holocaust Museum in Washington, DC. There you will find a room filled with human hair representing all the hair shaved off the heads of Jewish women in concentration camps. Let it stop you cold. Let it remind you of what the world thinks of women and their hair, their femininity, their bodies. Excuse yourself so that you can cry in the public bathroom.

Your hair will fall out by the handful after your first child is born. Do not be alarmed. Even though the shower drain is clogged and clumps of hair are everywhere, your hair will grow back. It will never be the same, though. It will be thinner, not nearly as shiny, and rather limp. Make peace with that.

Your second baby will nurse while holding a long strand of your hair in his hands. Because of this, it is important that you do not cut it, despite the fact that it is in your face. The moments you share with this child are precious. Your hair is part of your bonding experience.

When the first baby turns thirteen, you'll begin to find gray hairs in your own head every single day. At first it is funny, but don't laugh too hard. Soon you will have so many that you cannot count them or pluck them. Your mom and sister will laugh at you when you tell them you will not dye it or hide the gray in any way. Ignore them. But do consider readopting that Dorothy Hamill bob with a modern twist. It will likely be more flattering at forty-one than it was at four.

This time, instead of going to your mother, find a brand new hairdresser, one in the city, one who none of your friends know. In the waiting area stare at all the hair on the floor: blonde, purple, black, and brown locks, all ready to be swept out with the trash. These will remind you of an old folk belief that warns people not to throw hair from a brush or a fresh cut outside. The birds will gather it and use it for nests. They'll wind your hair in and out of twigs and grass, and this will make you go mad. You'll be helpless. Powerless. Insane. When you sit in the chair, ready for your dramatic new do, think of those birds and the hair on the floor. You will suddenly realize the power, the drama, the history of your hair. You will not be able to let that go—the baby twirling your tresses between chubby fingers, the lover watching you untangle your thick mane, your mother twisting perfect braids. Each strand is a page of your past. Tell the hairdresser, "Only a wee bit off the ends, please. I want to keep it long."

MAKE-UP BAG

I.

Pink Lemonade, Cherries
in the Snow, Red Alert, Sway,
Black Cherry, Feline, Sub-
versive Socialite . . .

So many blood hues, but
a few purple bruises
rattle around in there, too.

My daughter and I
are a lipstick coven
of two.

2.

If a crime lab swept
a Q-tip over Cherries in the Snow,
could they tell who used it last?

3.

I paint Red Alert on
my full bottom lip
(the one some people used to like to bite)
and I can tell that she used it yesterday.
My mouth tingles with her
I'm-sixteen-and-will-live-forever certainty.

4.

When she uses Feline does
she taste my crow's feet,
my disappointment,
my extra 30 pounds?

5.

Sometimes, she carelessly tosses
damp Kleenex imprinted with her lips
around the bathroom. Each tissue is
a sigil, a promise, a birthday wish.

I sweep them up and throw her kisses
in the trash bin, *Black Cherry*
staining my fingers.

I sneak one out—*Sway*— & fold it
neatly between the pages of her
photo album, next to baby
pictures and tender snippets of
downy hair & hospital bracelets.

6.
"I'm going out."

7.
The words flow over *Sub-
versive Socialite,* a red so

deep and dark, it is startling
against her complexion.

Pink Lemonade tells her to
"be careful, don't be late."

8.

When she is gone, I
wash off my lazy lip color

and apply the *Sub-
versive Socialite* she

left behind. It's all wrong.
Mattes don't work for me.

They crack & bleed around
my mouth, an open sore.
Today, *ChapStick* will be
good enough.

A LIST OF PICTURES I DIDN'T TAKE THIS SUMMER

the candid shot

my children, together, lounging on the grass while maple
leaves wave little hellos above their heads

the selfie

me crying because I've ruined a simple paint job in a tiny
bathroom; green paint plastering my hair to the side of my
face; eyes swollen, nose raw

the foodie pic

peach pie with a perfect lattice-topped crust dusted with
sugar, juices overflowing indecently over the crimped edge

the cute couple

a swipe of shaving cream on the back of the neck, a scrape
of a razor, a perfect line right above the collar; a kiss on the
head, a whisper in an ear

the new outfit

a candy apple red swimsuit with a halter neck and a ruched
bodice shoved in the back of a drawer, tags still neatly
affixed

the family vacation Christmas card photo

everyone huddled together on the bank of a river, mosqui-
toes pecking at exposed flesh, the dog whining, the kids
fighting, the fireworks thoroughly disappointing

the fancy yoga pose

the perfect headstand, in my PJs, heels almost (but not)
touching Stephen King on the bookshelf; hair in my eyes,
the sunlight filtering through the dusty blinds spotlighting
an ant on the carpet

the sporty outing

a great blue heron who is really my father just inches from
the kayak; the mist telling me my ghosts are everywhere;
the tiniest of turtles bubbling to the surface of the mucky
water to remind me I'm still actually here on this earth

the ladies night out

a fire, smoky sage, incantations in the dark; secret spells
and tinkling laughter rising to the clouds and circling the
moon

SWEET TOOTH

1. It started with pastel cigarettes called Fantasia by Nat Sherman, a high end cigarette first created in the 1950s for women to coordinate with their gowns. I'm not sure what prompted me to buy that first pack. I had never even seen them before the day I spied them in the window of the quaint downtown drugstore across the street from the university where I was a graduate student. Back in California, the liquor stores where I hurriedly bought smokes and gum before rushing to class carried only the basics: Lucky Strike, Kool, American Spirit, Camel. They certainly were more expensive than my usual Marlboro lights, but I was so fascinated that I made sure to buy Fantasias as often as I could.

When I was little my father never smoked cigarettes. Just, on occasion, a pipe. I'd go with him to the smoke shop where he'd buy tobacco laced with vanilla or cherry. The glass jars on the counter held different blends the way similar jars in a dime store might hold lemon drops or bon bons. The smoke was a thin, hazy blue and the scent intertwined with the tang of his Old Spice. The smell was comforting and sacred: a prayer.

Each of my fancy cigarettes was a different color: blush pink, robin's egg blue, light green, soft yellow—all tipped with a shiny gold filter. I don't recall the flavor being much different from a regular cigarette, maybe a bit lighter perhaps, smoother—though it would have been nice if they were flavored, so that they tasted sweet on the lips and tongue. I also remember wishing that the smoke matched the pretty paper, but it was the same deadly gray of any other cigarette.

Eight months before I started graduate school, my father collapsed and died after a massive heart attack at the bookstore. He was clutching a copy of Edith Wharton's Age of Innocence. No more Old Spice, no more cherry-blue incense smoke. I buried my head in his pillow and breathed in the last of him, hoping it would sustain me.

2. There was a candy shop just a few doors down from the drugstore, and when I wasn't buying Easter egg cigarettes, I was buying sugar to take back to my apartment. Brightly colored jellies and marzipans, Turkish delight, Jordan almonds, and butter mints lured me in.

My ex-boyfriend liked me to be thin, suggested I go to the gym and turned me from side to side to size up my hips. He embraced the 1990s "Grunge" look and never cut his hair and wore old thrift-store flannels and Vans. He preferred, though, that I wear short, cheerleader style skirts. That was his thing.

I examined every item in that candy store and was overjoyed when the selection changed with the season: candy corn became candy canes, which turned to conversation hearts; eventually, marshmallow chicks replaced them all. Every day was a celebration, a holiday, a reason to be joyful.

For Valentine's Day the previous year that same boyfriend bought me a book: an academic study of Irish folklore. I really wanted a heart-shaped box of chocolates, the kind with lace and a big bow on the lid. He knew that was what I craved, but he "didn't believe in Hallmark holidays."

3. Night after night that first year in grad school, I had vivid dreams of storefronts displaying the most colorful delicacies: a vendor selling Mexican conchas paired with hot chocolate, an ice cream counter with hundreds of rainbow flavors, bakeries pedaling pies, oozing hot fruit juices over their crusty edges. One particular cake made an appearance several different times. It was a cake so perfectly decorated with yellow and white frosting that it looked like porcelain, a Wedgewood jewelry box. Piped edges and stiff sugar-roses beckoned. But I never had a chance to eat a slice of that dream cake. I never even ran a finger through the icing to taste the heady sweetness. It was always behind the glass of a shop window, and, just as I was about to enter, something would pull me away. It could be a voice calling my name from across the street, or the chiming of a clock tower reminding me to hurry to class.

The definition of tantalizing according to Merriam-Webster Dictionary: Possessing a quality that arouses or stimulates desire or interest; also: mockingly or teasingly out of reach; derived from the Greek story of Tantalus."

It wasn't just the cake that was out of reach. I never got my hands on the conchas, the ice cream, or the pies. Sometimes, I would open my wallet to pay for my goodies, only to find I had no money at all. Or, as I walked up to the counter to order, the cashier would tell me the bakery just closed, come back later.

Zeus punished Tantalus for his crimes (stealing ambrosia being one of them) by banishing him to the depths of the underworld. Above his head a tree branch laden with ripe fruit dangled, just out of reach. The wind blew the branch away from his grasp every time he tried to pluck the magical fruit. He stood in a crystal pool of water, yet, when he would lean down to quench his thirst with a sip, the waters receded, leaving his lips dry and his throat aching for comfort.

4. I woke up with a start today. It's been almost twenty-one years now, but the dream is eerily familiar. This time I was late for a train but needed to stop at a sweets shop to pick up candy for a party. The interior was like an old-fashioned ice cream parlor complete with marble countertops and cheery jars of penny candy. I stood in the store and hurriedly jammed candy in bags. This time, while the sweets were inviting, I didn't feel like I wanted them, not really. I had other things to do and wanted to leave. The shop owner tried to persuade me to get a few more sugared orange slices and didn't I want some root beer barrels, too? In a huff I left all the candy on the counter top and ran for the train. Other, better, things were waiting for me.

The man in my life these days is loving and kind, so unlike that thoughtless boy of my younger days. I have children with him, too, and these teens love candy just like their mother. They count their change and walk to the Dollar General. They come back with peanut butter cups and chocolate kisses or perhaps a pocket full of Jolly Ranchers. I try, in a small way, to stop them. Think of your teeth! I won't allow it until after you eat some vegetables! But it is all show.

I want them to have a sweet life.

WINGS

My friend Deb and I decided to take a trip to Mexico last winter. She had been once before, but I'd never visited. Instead of hitting the beaches and wild tourist spots popular with American travelers we decided to travel inland to Puebla. Our first excursion was to Cholula and the San Gabrial Friary.

The back door of the church itself was mustard yellow, clean, and rich under the cloudless sky. The Spanish Order of Friar Minors established the church in 1529. It was built upon a temple to Quetzalcoatl, a fierce and feathered serpent god and principal deity of the Aztecs. Quetzalcoatl was the god of the wind and of the dawn, of wisdom and knowledge.

Mass was in progress that morning, so Deb and I didn't go in. Instead, we strolled outside and explored the grounds and examined the graves with their crumbling names and headstones flaking with age. I marveled at the brutal blue sky. My limbs were buzzing, electric with anticipation of the day ahead.

THE NAUHA BELIEVED THAT "TONALLI" WAS A PORTION OF ONE'S SOUL THAT WAS VITAL TO A PROPERLY FUNCTIONING ENERGETIC BODY. IT WAS SEEN AS "AN ANIMATING SACRED ENERGY THAT DIFFUSED OVER AND ENERGIZED THE EARTH AND ITS INHABITANTS."[1]

93

Next, we headed to the Great Pyramid of Cholula or Tlachihualtepetl. This, too, was a temple dedicated to Quetzalcoatl though much older than the one destroyed by the Spanish in order to erect San Gabriel. By the time the colonists arrived it was overgrown and simply looked like a large and looming hill. The locals knew, though, that the area was sacred, and they continued to bury their dead at the perimeter. Archaeologists began exploration of the pyramid in the 1930s, and today over five miles of tunnels honeycomb the site underneath the church.

We were eager to see the ruins of the pyramid. But, in order to reach the outdoor archaeological site, we had to enter through one of the underground tunnels.

"What does that sign say?" I asked Deb after buying our tickets. She spoke fluent Spanish and I, despite my Mexican heritage, did not.

"It says, 'do not enter if afraid of small spaces.'"

The entryway to the tunnel was narrow and really only able to accommodate visitors in a single file line rather than side by side. Yellow lights illuminated the stone and dirt. The cool air was welcome after the midday heat of the church courtyard. But, after only a few feet the three people in front of us turned abruptly. Two men guided a middle-age woman back to the entrance as she hunched over crying. Her companion lifted his head and simply said, "Claustrofobia."

I didn't need Deb to translate.

SUSTO: A TYPE OF SPIRITUAL "SHOCK" CAUSED BY UPSETTING NEWS, A SUDDEN FRIGHT, OR A BAD SCARE.

THE ANCIENT NUAHA PEOPLE ALSO HAD A NAME FOR A GREAT FRIGHT: TETONALCAUALTILIZTLI. TETONALCAUALTILIZTLI CAN RESULT IN THE PARTIAL LOSS OF ONE'S TONALLI. [2]

We continued forward into the tunnel.

"I don't like this," Deb whispered.

I shrugged and assured her that this was no big deal, it was interesting in there, and I bet it wouldn't be long until we were out.

After a minute of silence, Deb asked, "Have you ever seen The Descent?

That was it. One mention of the 2005 movie about a group of explorers lost in a system of underground caves in North Carolina, and I was a goner. I imagined the rocky ceilings collapsing and crushing us, pressing our lungs and smashing our limbs as we struggled to breathe, to escape.

I'd dealt with panic attacks my whole adult life, some so bad I was convinced of imminent death based on the racing of my heart. But the one I experienced at that moment almost brought me to my knees. I moved forward, though, Deb right behind me.

Breathe, breathe, breathe. . .

I repeated this over and over in my head as I picked up the pace. We weren't running but we moved as if we were in training for a speed walking race.

Just. Fucking. Breathe. . .

We couldn't see the end. There was only turn after turn as we willed the sunshine to find us, guide us to the open air we knew awaited.

And then we saw it: the exit. We'd been walking for maybe ten minutes, but it felt like hours. At this point we did run. We stumbled outside into the white bright glow of the noonday sun. My legs, flooded with adrenaline, shook violently, and we both leaned over gulping the fresh air into our hungry mouths.

We got our bearings and calmed ourselves enough to continue to the archaeological site. Unlike the shady tunnels, the grounds of the temple ruins were hot and dry. A portion of the temple steps were exposed at the base of the hill. We sat on the lowest step and drank water until our bottles were almost empty. A few people walked past us on the way to the top, but the altitude was already challenging our lungs and we hesitated. Yet there was an undeniable draw towards the sun, and together we started the climb. Part way up, Deb decided to head back and rest at the bottom of the steps. I kept moving knowing that if I turned and looked down, vertigo would set in.

I kept my eyes on the steps and my hand on the rope that served as a handrail. Up and up I went. The threat of crushing death that I felt below the temple transmuted into exhilaration. Each step was a step closer to the heavens.

"THERE WERE MANY RITES SHAMAN USED TO RESTORE THE TONALLI. ONE COMMON PRACTICE WAS TO GARNER THE HELP OF THE SUN." [3]

At the top, I looked down and imagined tumbling head over tail down the stone until I crashed to the dirt, broken. But I shook the vision free and lifted my head to take in the sights of Cholula. The city spread all around me like liquid metal, oozing and shimmery. Then I looked up to that cloudless sky again and grew wings. I stood upon tiptoes and shrugged my shoulders to feel feathers push through my shirt. I opened my mouth and swallowed the sun until my chest burned with its heat. As I soared and swooped, Deb waved goodbye and wished me luck in my journey. I plucked a feather from the back of my neck and let it float into her waiting hand.

[1]*Curanderismo: Soul Retrieval*, page 20, Erika Buenaflor, Bear & Company 2019

[2] *Healing with Herbs and Rituals*, Eliseo Torres, University of New Mexico Press 2006

[3] García, J.E. (2014). Tonalli, cold nature, and fearful personality: Susto among sixteenth century Nahuas. Estudios de Cultura Nahuatl. 48. 177-212.

Thank you:

I'd like to thank the following people for their support:
Paul Moyer, Ethan Moyer, Bridget Moyer, Michael Benson,
Deb Sperling, Robin Flanigan, Annette Daniels Taylor,
Annette Ramos, Sandy Bourdeau, Jeanette Colby, Kelly
Myers, Karen Faris, Jennie Barnett, Dan Varenka, Veronica
Green, Lorraine Lucero Green Hagler, Michele Ashlee-
Meade, Courtney Smith, and Karen Stein.
And thank you to those who have passed but had a pro-
found influence on my life or writing: Robert Green, Mary
Cordova, Sylvia Joggerst, and M.J. Iuppa.

Christine Green is a writer in Western New York.
Learn more at christinejgreen.com

Sweet Tooth | Christine Green

Copyright © 2024 Christine Green

ISBN: 979-8-218-46999-3

Second Printing | Fall 2024

Zaftig Press | Rochester, NY
zaftigpress.com